HOW TO DATE THE GIRL YOU'VE ALWAYS DESIRED

DATE THE GIRL YOU'VE ALWAYS DREAMT OF HAVING BUT DIDN'T DARE ASK

JOY MARCUS

Contents

CHAPTER ONE

WHAT WOMEN WANT

What do women want? This question that has been a mystery to men from time immemorial and we are not closer to understanding women than we do when playing soccer and hockey.

Why are women so hard to decode? They are hard to decipher because we try to understand them with a man's eye without understanding that women think differently and see differently. Unless we understand they way they think, we will never be able to understand them on a logical level.

For instance, what do we do when we get together for some fun? We evidently do not share feelings. Instead, we drink, talk about sports and do other things. It is natural for guys.

On the other hand, when women get together they share their feelings, talk about the latest fashion, hair style or diet. So, you see, men thrive on competition, adrenaline, power, domination, logic and structure in our lives, while women do not care about them. They thrive by emotion.

If you actually want to be able to date any girl, no matter how ugly or attractive she is, you have to know what drives her, the things that please her and her motives. Take note, many women are not conscious of drives them or what their motives are; it's just the way nature has made them.

Nevertheless, just as you need to know what interests her, you should not worry about it making sense because it may not make sense to we guys because we see things differently, don't forget that. Therefore, if you know what her buttons are, you will be able to play sweet music that she won't be able to resist.

You like power, don't you? Knowledge is power, and it comes by learning, so, learn what drives women and then you will have the power to date the woman of your choice.

CHAPTER TWO

WHAT THEY SAY THEY WANT

You have to note that there is a big difference between what women say they want and what they actually respond to. For example, most women will say they want a dependable, nice guy who will treat them well. That's a good wish, but then, why are so many women attracted to bad guys? Why do we see so many beautiful women dating guys with the 'bad boy appearance'?

The reason is not farfetched, and that is because what women say they want and what they really want are two very different things. What they say they want has a lot to do with the way society has conditioned them to think, while nature determines the type of guys that actually attracts them. Normally, nature wins the society.

"Are you actually saying I should be a bad guy?" You may ask. The answer is 'Yes and No'. Confusing right? I know, but this is what I mean. Women are actually attracted to men that are strong, courageous, confident, and not the "nice guys" who do everything but lick asses and the floor they walk on.

I want to give you and assignment; take a look at those romance novels women love so much and try and find one where the guy is "nice." I wish you long journey because you're going to be looking forever, as most of the men in these romance novels are tough, courageous and powerful.

And do you know what? Women love those books for a reason, and that's because they wish to have such kind of men as depicted in the novel.

It is unfortunate that it seems society has shaped men over the past few decades that men are expected to be even more sensitive than women. The problem is that while women liked such men, they are only really interested in them as friends.

The good news is that it's actually okay to be a man that is courageous, strong, confident since women love to see such traits in a man.

ATTRACTION

Attraction is another necessary element that determines whether or not you get a date. Don't be intimidated by that; the good news is that women are more attracted to personality than they are to looks. Looks do play some role in attraction, but if you have the right personality traits, women will still be attracted to you.

Therefore, if your excuse until now has been that you aren't rich or famous, then you have to realize that it is only an excuse. While women may be attracted to the rich and famous, personality still wins out. No matter the amount of cash you have in your bank account if you have the confidence and humor that women love, you will win every time.

Having the ability to attract women is not an inherited trait; it's something you can learn. Therefore, you can make yourself more attractive to women by cultivating the type of personalities they would be attracted to.

If you think that you don't have to change to make a woman attracted to you, but prefer she love you for who you are, I think you should wake up from your dream and face reality because everyone has to change, and change, is the only thing that is constant in life. We either allow life to mold us, change us, and give us what we don't' want to get, or we channel the change to get what we want to get.

However, an attraction is not a choice. It's not as if a woman will see a guy, study him, write down his qualities, and then choose whether or not to be attracted to him. It doesn't work that way; if it did, then you probably wouldn't want to read this book.

Attraction is entirely biological. What this means is that if she wasn't attracted to you after your first date, there is little you could do about it because you will likely never be anything more than a friend to her. It will be better you go on with your life because no matter how many gifts you buy for her or how many restaurants you take her to, she is not going to suddenly develop an attraction for you.

BECOMING MORE ATTRACTIVE TO WOMEN

The mistake most men do when they are around attractive women, they try to gain their approval by being overly nice, careful and so on; this puts the woman in the position to lead, and if she is the one leading out, she will never feel that spark of attraction for you. Remember what I said before, women are attracted to strong and confident men, and a strong guy lead and not the other way round.

The best way to spark that fire of attraction is to make her work for your attention, and not for you to seek her approval by being too nice and careful. This trick unbalances her cool and makes here curious about you, because you are doing something unexpected and out of the ordinary, so, she will be interested in knowing you better.

Confidence is very attractive to both women and men, therefore, the more you look like you don't need her approval and attention, the more confident you will appear before her. The more confident you can act in every situation, the more attractive you will be.

Meanwhile, be careful not to cross the line because there is a fine line between confidence and arrogance. Arrogance may be good to a certain degree, but too much of it will make you look repulsive.

CHAPTER FIVE

THE EXCUSE

Many guys always give reasons they failed with women, but most of the time that excuse is merely in their heads. The reason many guys fail to get the woman they want is because of the way they think, which impacts on their behavior.

Let's take for instance, when you see and attractive woman and think that you will never have a chance at talking to her, then, your actions will be in line with your thoughts. You would probably not dare approach her, and if you do, you will give off a "scared" vibe.

On the other way round, the more confident you are in your abilities to win and attract a woman, the stronger you appear and the more attractive you will be. In many occasions, the shortcomings we imagine we have stopped us from acting, and sometimes we don't even realize we have them in our psyche.

To overcome this problem, you have to do a little soul searching. You have to identify the excuses that have been holding you back so that you can deal with it. Then the next thing is to educate yourself about women to know what sparks that feeling of attraction in them.

As soon as you understand what women desire, then you will be able to project an aura of strength that they will find irresistible. It may interest you to know that every woman has a little girl inside of her longing for protection and care and that little girl is the one who will have the final word. If you understand that little girl, speak to her and show her you are in control of every aspect of your life, then, the woman will be attracted to you, and engulf you like a flame.

It's crucial that you accept the fact that the power to improve and attract a woman is within you. Ignore excuses such as "am not handsome, am not rich, am not this, am not that". Stop the self-pity and start to understand that if you can make a woman feel good, you will win out over any guy with a Ferrari if he has the personality of a wet rag – that's just how it is.

CHAPTER SIX

NICE GUYS VS BAD BOYS

It is very annoying to the nice guys when they see that the bad boys always get the girls. Why? It is so because while the 'nice guy' is trying to wine and dine her, and kiss her backside and handle her with kid gloves for fear of upsetting her, the bad boy couldn't care less what she thinks about him, or what anyone thinks.

Bad boys project an aura of danger and power that women are attracted to because they don't care what anyone thinks – or pretend not to care because they are in control.

Bad boys project 'strength' and 'strong man' which women love, and that's why women fall head over heels for them. The problem is that most of these guys turn out to be abusive jerks later on in the relationship, yet most beautiful women still love them and can let go of them, even when the guy beats them up.

Ironically, on the other hand, some women see the nice guy as being dishonest or hypocritical because they usually ignore their needs and desires to please a woman, making the woman think the guy is nice simply because he wants something from her or because he is not confident in himself. So, he's either a pussy or a hypocrite, neither of which attracts women.

To be that perfect guy, you have to combine the best of both worlds, namely projecting the "bad boy" power while never becoming abusive or controlling. The interesting this about this is that you can learn to project the same aura of power. Just believe that you can, and also, be willing to work on building your confidence levels, and then you will be the best man for the woman.

CHAPTER SEVEN

PERSONALITY TRAITS WOMEN FIND IRRESISTIBLE

Your personality is your most powerful asset to make a woman feel good. A woman will be attracted and stay attracted to a man who makes her feel good when she is with him or thinking of him. There are certain personality traits that you can cultivate which women find completely irresistible.

For instance, one of the things women like is a man with a good sense of humor. The truth is that the more you can make her laugh, the more she will desire to spend time with you. Women are also attracted to intelligent men, especially those who know how to use that intelligence to surprise and engage her.

Women love to listen to stories about people or places, so, education is another powerful weapon you can use. If you are knowledgeable on many issues, you will always have a topic to talk about, you will be able to talk about something interesting that engages her instead of the usual boring topics most guys talk about, like her favorite color or where she works, or her favorite food.

Dominance is another thing women love; they are attracted to dominant men, even if they don't realize it; this is how they have been structured biologically, women seek the protection of a male, and the more dominant the man is, the better the chance he has of protecting her. Once again, there is a line, don't mistake being dominant with being controlling or troublesome. You need to dominate the challenges in your life rather than being controlling of hers and taking away her individuality and happiness.

Men who are very thoughtful are also very attractive to women. You see, when you give a woman a gift, she will not be overjoyed because of the gift itself but because it is a proof that you were thinking of her. The gift is an indication that you were thinking about her, and the thought of that makes her feel good, even if it is to tell her you weren't happy that she was flirting with another guy.

For you to impress a woman, then you need to learn to notice details. Women spend a lot of time making sure they look good, so if she has a beautiful hairdo or wears that hot dress, it wasn't an accident. She is just trying to impress you, and if you notice these details and commend her, she will be happy that you noticed her attempts to be attractive to you, and that will make her feel good staying around you.

Women also like aggressive men, but not in the manner that you won't take no for an answer. That's called date rape, and it will spoil everything.

The kind of aggressive men women like is those who know exactly what they want in life, go after it with everything they have, and won't stop until they achieve it.

Confidence combined with humor is the right attitude. This means that you are so confident that you laugh at yourself without feeling insecure or intimidated.

CHAPTER EIGHT

INSECURITY IS THE BIGGEST TURN OFF

Insecurity is one of the biggest obstacles men face. It is the main thing that will make you completely unattractive. Women can smell insecurity and neediness immediately, and there's nothing that will turn her off quite quickly as much as an insecure guy. Seriously.

If you feel uncomfortable in a given situation or with who you are, you will become insecure. An 'insecure' man may try to appear confident, but his words will fetch him out. Some example of insecurity includes allowing others to make the decisions. Women like it when men make the decision and then they only follow. If she wants to do something else, she will tell you but don't always expect her to make the decisions. If you depend on her to make decisions on what you will do or where you will go, she will feel you are insecure.

Arguing about everything is another way you come off as being insecure. Even if you are right, you will appear insecure when you argue with every little thing just to prove you are right, and she's wrong.

She will also think you are insecure if you start crowding her or being too touchy-feely from the beginning. You need to restrain yourself a little and let her become comfortable with you. If you are always touching her, she will either think that you are afraid she is going to run away, or you only want to get her into bed, and then you disappear.

CHAPTER NINE

WOMEN AND SEX

Do you know that women love sex just as much as men? Society has simply made it a taboo topic, but the truth of the matter is that women enjoy sex and talk about it with their girlfriends all the time, and they are magnetically drawn to a man who is skillful in making love.

It is not easy to find a guy who knows how to please a woman in bed, as most guys are quite selfish in this department. When it comes to sexual pleasure, women are different from men, their mind needs to be involved just as much as their body. Most guys just rush through the process, without acknowledging that it takes much more than penetration to please women in bed.

The word 'foreplay' needs to be branded embedded into your brain because if you get the foreplay right, women will be satisfied. You will end up having to push them off because they will keep needing more.

Foreplay is more than sex; it's about well-placed touches, softly telling her what you would like to be doing to her even though you are in public place, it's about setting the mood and building the anticipation. All these little details get her imagination fired up and wanting more. The more sexual tension and anticipation you build, the quicker she will melt in your arms.

You may ask, "How this affects your ability to date any girl?" Women are masters at reading body language, so they pick up on things like this quickly. And a man who knows exactly how to please a woman exhibits a certain confidence that feels like, "I am going to rock your world," and women can pick up on that too.

You will not only become very attractive to women by becoming a master at pleasing women, but you will also maintain that attraction because a skilled lover is a rare commodity and they won't want to let you go.

CHAPTER TEN

APPEARANCE

Women are very much attracted to personality than looks, but this doesn't mean you shouldn't make yourself presentable. If you wear a pair of jeans that looks bad, with you looking like you are nine months pregnant; you will find out that attractive women will not give you a second glance. This is so because women make a lot of decisions based on every small detail. For instance, if you are too casually dressed then she will think you are too lazy to look after yourself, and if that is true, you would probably have a dirty home, and that would probably present too much work for her to do when she settles with you.

On the other end hand, if you overdo your appearance and look too put-together, she will think you will be spending more time taking care of yourself than you would take care of her. It may be a little tricky to strike the balance, but as long as you take good care of yourself, and that includes losing the beer belly, women will be attracted to you. You should just pick up a magazine, select a few new designs of clothes and that's okay.

It is a fact that women take the time to make themselves attractive to men, and it does take them a lot of time and work; therefore, they expect the same consideration in return, which is natural. Do a moderate gym and get yourself in shape which will not only help you more success with women but will also make you healthier which means you'll have more years to enjoy life with good health.

CHAPTER ELEVEN

WHY SHOULD I CHANGE?

Well, no one is forcing you to change if you don't want to. But it is worth the effort if you want to be able to date any girl, no matter how attractive she is. I want you to know that we do not live in a perfect world, so if you want her to love you for who you are, then you are going to have a big problem.

So many men approach women that are very attractive, and this makes the women use the outer appearance of a man to decide whether or not he is worth her time. They will judge the type of person you are based on your appearance, and they will hardly want to spend a chance to look beyond an overweight and ungroomed appearance as well as a total lack of culture. They start with your presentation before every other thing follow.

Another angle of it is that it's also a matter of self-respect. Not wanting to improve means not having respect for yourself. Have a shower every day, get your hair trimmed, go to the gym, read a few books, browse the internet and learn a little about what's trending, and suddenly you will find that your confidence will be boosted, and you will start exhibiting the right attitude.

CHAPTER TWELVE

FEAR OF FAILURE

Many men will walk into a dangerous situation without a second thought, whereas they are paralyzed by the mere thought of talking to an attractive woman because we are afraid of being rejected. This inability to take action is one of the biggest problems men have. We are simply paralyzed by the fear of rejection so much that we would rather not take any action at all.

Think about it. We are not afraid to engage in a fight even when we know that we are going to experience some physical pain and bruises, yet we are more afraid of approaching an attractive woman, even when we know that the worst that can happen is that she will say no, which will not remove anything from us. So don't be afraid of failure.

WHERE TO MEET WOMEN

Finding where to meet women is not as hard as you might think. Start by going to the same places they go, and that doesn't mean just going down to the pub for a pint.

You have first to decide on what type of woman you would like to date. For instance, you might want a woman who is into working out, so then you should join a gym. Go out to clubs if you are looking for a party girl, and so on. However, do remember that there are lots of guys vying for their attention in settings like bars.

You just have to sit down, look around, and think about where your ideal type of woman would likely hang out and then start going there. Women also love the idea of "accidentally" meeting a man in a normal but unexpected place. The grocery store, bookstore or malls are some good examples where you can meet them.

Places you can meet women are virtually uncountable. You just have to use intelligence and creativity a little bit to get the kind of woman you need.

CHAPTER FOURTEEN

HOW TO MEET WOMEN

Women don't really respond all that well to a pick-up line, and they can smell it a mile away. The issue is that while you might be a genuine guy, she will simply think that you are either a player or weak. Smooth pick-up lines always turn on the alarm bells for most women because they believe they are being played. The fact that she may have been told by many other guys how beautiful she is won't help the situation much either. Therefore, the key is to stand out from the crowd and be real.

Women are like predators when it comes to sensing your weaknesses and your intentions. They can sense what you want from a distance because they are masters at reading body language. So Don't EVER presume they don't have any idea of what you are doing because it's a game you will not win. You will give yourself away before you even utter the first syllable and then your mission is doomed to fail.

Therefore, instead of hiding the fact that you are attempting to pick her up, get great at it and you will not have to hide anymore. Remember, confidence and humor is a powerful combination that you can use to your advantage in achieving your goal.

CHAPTER FIFTEEN

DOWN WITH PICK UP LINES, UP WITH CONVERSATION

One of the challenges with pick up lines is that they are a clear sign that you are nervous. The delivery is much more crucial than what you actually say. For example, whether or not you recite the telephone book, she would still find you attractive if you are relaxed and confident. On the other hand, you will not win any point if you stutter over a pre-rehearsed pick-up line, this will show that you are nervous.

More so, rather than starting off with some pick-up line, your chances would increase tenfold if you engage her in a captivating and exciting topic, asking her opinion. She will be more likely to answer because women don't like to be rude for the sake of it. Also, it's an excellent way to draw her into a lengthier conversation which allows her to know you better. It will work very well if you request her opinion on a controversial subject you are debating with a friend.

If you just ask whether you can buy her a drink or not, she might say "No, thanks," and then leave. However, if you tell her that you've been arguing with your friend on whether women earn less than what men earn doing the same job, and that you need her opinion, this will spark her interest, and she will likely stick around and argue her point.

CHAPTER SIXTEEN

THE PHONE NUMBER OR EMAIL ADDRESS

Most women love giving out their email than they are their phone number. Fortunately, email is a much better way to start off the communication because they are a little distant compared to on the phone. So communication is easier.

Using email will make her more comfortable with you as she will gain a little insight into how you reason. She will also be delighted that you took the time to think about you should say to her. Another advantage of email is that you are more likely to reach her than by calling her, and she would likely to answer an email. Another benefit of email is that, unlike the phone, with email, she can answer at any time because she may not be able to answer calls at work or in a crucial meeting.

The best way to ask for a phone number or an email address is to use little humor and confidence. For example, you can ask here whether she has email or not. When she answers yes, simply take out a piece of paper and pen and pass them to her, essentially taking her 'yes' as an acceptance to give it to you, she will hardly resist.

Then, while she is writing you may try to get her to write down her number as well, or, just wait to get her number later via email. You know, being harassed by email is quite unlikely, so women see little risk in giving out their email. You will be better off exchanging few emails first, and then, ask her for her number via mail.

Remember to remain confident when asking for her email. So, to build up your confidence, just practice getting phone numbers and emails from women, in the mall every day so you can get over your fear of rejection. The more rejections you receive, the less they will affect you. That's a secret.

CHAPTER SEVENTEEN

CONCLUSION

If you truly want to be able to date any girl, no matter how attractive she is, then you have to cultivate the personality traits that she finds attractive. It is true that some guys are born with these traits; they can also be learned, and since women are much more attracted to a man's personality and the way he makes her feel than his looks, nothing is blocking your success other than yourself – acquire the personality traits.

You have to eliminate your limiting beliefs; you have to understand that the constant thing in life is 'change'. If you do that, your confidence will grow, and you will be much more attractive to women. A woman will happily go out with an average-looking guy that has a mediocre financial solution than to go out with a rich, great looking guy if the former makes her feel wonderful while the latter acts like a joke.

Finally, I want you to know that the only thing standing between you and success with women is you. Yes, you! Learn to be more attractive to women following the guides in this book, and you will find out that nothing can stand in your way; learn the personality traits, and appear neat.

Disclaimer

Introduction

By using this book, you accept this disclaimer in full.

No advice

The book contains information. The information is not advice and should not be treated as such.

No representations or warranties

To the maximum extent permitted by applicable law and subject to section below, we exclude all representations, warranties, undertakings and guarantees relating to the book.

Without prejudice to the generality of the foregoing paragraph, we do not represent, warrant, undertake or guarantee:

- that the information in the book is correct, accurate, complete or non-misleading.

- that the use of the guidance in the book will lead to any particular outcome or result.

Limitations and exclusions of liability

The limitations and exclusions of liability set out in this section and elsewhere in this disclaimer: are subject to section 6 below; and govern all liabilities arising under the disclaimer or in relation to the book, including liabilities arising in contract, in tort (including negligence) and for breach of statutory duty.

We will not be liable to you in respect of any losses arising out of any event or events beyond our reasonable control.

We will not be liable to you in respect of any business losses, including without limitation loss of or damage to profits, income, revenue, use, production, anticipated savings, business, contracts, commercial opportunities or goodwill.

We will not be liable to you in respect of any loss or corruption of any data, database or software.

We will not be liable to you in respect of any special, indirect or consequential loss or damage.

Exceptions

Nothing in this disclaimer shall: limit or exclude our liability for death or personal injury resulting from negligence; limit or exclude our liability for fraud or fraudulent misrepresentation; limit any of our liabilities in any way that is not permitted under applicable law; or exclude any of our liabilities that may not be excluded under applicable law.

Severability

If a section of this disclaimer is determined by any court or other competent authority to be unlawful and/ or unenforceable, the other sections of this disclaimer continue in effect.

If any unlawful and/or unenforceable section would be lawful or enforceable if part of it were deleted, that part will be deemed to be deleted, and the rest of the section will continue in effect.

Law and jurisdiction

This disclaimer will be governed by and construed in accordance with Swiss law, and any disputes relating to this disclaimer will be subject to the exclusive jurisdiction of the courts of Switzerland.

www.ingramcontent.com/pod-product-compliance
Lightning Source LLC
Chambersburg PA
CBHW051135250726
48655CB00007B/3080